RED-EYED TREE FROG

Story by

Joy Cowley

Illustrated with photographs by

Nic Bishop

Scholastic Press
New York

Evening comes to the rain forest.

The macaw
and the toucan
will soon go to sleep.

But the red-eyed tree frog
has been asleep all day.

It wakes up hungry.
What will it eat?

Here is an iguana.
Frogs do not eat iguanas.

Do iguanas eat frogs?
The red-eyed tree frog
does not wait to find out.

It hops onto
another branch.

The frog is hungry
but it will not eat the ant.

It will not eat
the katydid.

No!
The caterpillar is poisonous.

Will it eat the caterpillar?

Something moves
near the frog.

Something slips and slithers
along a branch.
It is a hungry boa snake.

The snake flicks its tongue.
It tastes frog in the air.
Look out, frog!

JUMP!

**The frog lands on a leaf,
far away from the boa.**

What does the frog
see on the leaf?

A moth!

The tree frog is
no longer hungry.

It climbs
onto a leaf.

The red-eyed tree frog shuts its eyes . . .

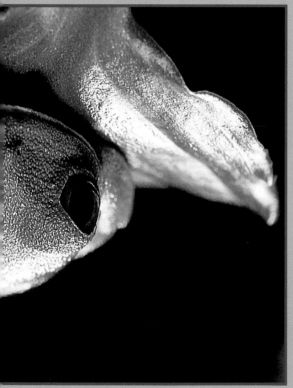

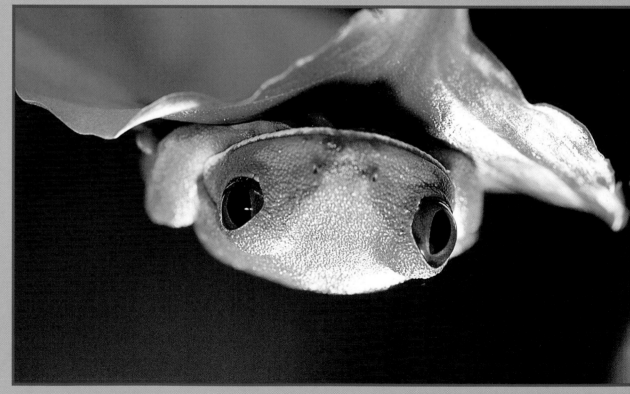

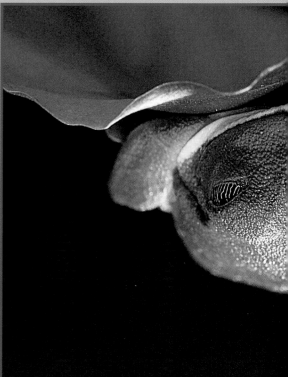

as morning comes to the rain forest.

DID YOU KNOW?

Red-eyed tree frogs live in the swampy parts of rain forests in Central America. They wake up just as the sun is going down and sit in the branches calling to one another. Their call sounds like, *"Gluck. Gluck. Gluck."*

In many pictures in this book, the red-eyed tree frog looks quite big. Really it is very small, its body only about two inches long. These two pages show the red-eyed tree frog at its actual size.

Tree frogs spend most of their lives in trees. They even lay their eggs in the trees. The female frog glues her eggs onto the underside of leaves that hang over water. Here the eggs are safe from other animals. When the tadpoles hatch, they drop into the water, where they feed and grow until they turn into baby frogs. Then they are ready to leave the water and climb up nearby plants.

Special suckers on the tree frog's toes help it climb and cling to leaves. The red-eyed tree frog also has large eyes to help it see in the dark and look for food. It likes to eat insects, but it has to be very careful. Many insects in the rain forest can defend themselves against hungry animals like frogs. Ants can bite, so they are best left alone. Katydids are often big and have lots of spines, so they are hard to swallow. Many caterpillars defend themselves by being poisonous. Moths, flies, spiders, and small grasshoppers are the tree frog's favorite foods.

Of course, the red-eyed tree frog also has to watch out that it doesn't become dinner for some other animal. A hungry bat might swoop down and snatch it from its perch. Or a snake like the baby boa in this book may sneak up on it. The tree frog's green color helps it blend in with its background, making it harder to find. A red-eyed tree frog will darken in color when it is frightened.

Before daylight returns, the red-eyed tree frog finds a hiding place among the leaves of the trees. It tucks its toes under its chin and belly, and flattens its body against a leaf. When it closes its eyes to sleep, only its green back is left showing. It stays hidden until it is ready to wake up again the next evening.

Library of Congress Cataloging-in-Publication Data
Cowley, Joy.
Red-eyed tree frog / by Joy Cowley;
photographs by Nic Bishop. — 1st ed.   p.   cm.
Summary: This frog found in the rain forest of Central America
spends the night searching for food while also being careful
not to become dinner for some other animal.
ISBN 0-590-87175-7
1. Hylidae — Central America — Juvenile literature.
[1. Tree frogs. 2. Frogs.] I. Bishop, Nic, 1955– ill. II. Title.
QL668.E24C685 1999   597.8'7 — dc21 98-15674
CIP   AC

10 9 8 7 6 5 4 3 2 1   9/9 0/0 01 02 03

Book design by David Caplan
The text type was set in 27-point Myriad 565 Condensed.

Printed in Singapore 46
First edition, March 1999

The photographer used original high-speed photographic
techniques to capture the images that appear in this book.